Dear Reader,

I know that sometimes the journey of studying can feel like an uphill climb, filled with challenges and moments of doubt. But I want you to remember this: every step you take, every page you read, and every concept you grasp is a step closer to your dreams and your goals.

Studying can be tough, but it's also a powerful tool that empowers you to unlock your potential and make a difference in the world. So, when you feel like giving up, take a deep breath and remind yourself why you started this journey in the first place.

You have within you an incredible reservoir of knowledge, creativity, and resilience. You are capable of achieving remarkable things, and each study session is a testament to your dedication and determination.

When you encounter difficult subjects or complex problems, don't be discouraged. These are the moments when you are growing the most, expanding your horizons, and building your mental strength. Embrace challenges as opportunities to learn and become better.

Remember, it's not about being the best; it's about being your best. Progress may be gradual, but every small victory is a step forward. So, celebrate your achievements, no matter how minor they may seem. They all contribute to your success.

Surround yourself with positivity and people who

uplift you. Seek help and guidance when you need it; there's no shame in asking for support. Together, we can accomplish more than we ever could alone.

Believe in yourself and your abilities. Visualize your goals and the life you're working towards. Let that vision be your driving force, your North Star, guiding you through the darkest nights of doubt.

You've got this! Stay focused, stay dedicated, and remember that every moment you invest in your studies brings you closer to the future you've always dreamed of. Keep your head high, keep pushing forward, and never forget that you are capable of greatness.

Believe in yourself, because I certainly believe in you.

With unwavering support,

Lia

Tip: Rip out the pages with the quotes that resonate with you and hang them in a place where you can always see them.

Write notes and your thoughts directly in the book so you can read them again and again.

"The only limits that exist are the ones you place on yourself."

- Rob Dyrdek

Tip: Challenge your own limitations and push your boundaries. You are capable of achieving more than you might think.

"Study while others are sleeping; work while others are loafing; prepare while others are playing, and dream while others are wishing."

- William A. Ward

"One day, all your hard work will pay off."

- Unknown

"I think it's possible for ordinary people to choose to be extraordinary."

- Elon Musk

"Don't wish it were easier; wish you were better."

- Jim Rohn, entrepreneur and motivational speaker

"A river cuts through rock not because of its power but because of its persistence."

- Unknown

"Every morning you have two choices:
continue to sleep with your dreams, or wake up
and chase them."

- Unknown

"Nobody can go back and start a new beginning, but anyone can start today and make a new ending."

- Maria Robinson

"Success is not final, failure is not fatal; it is the courage to continue that counts."

- Winston Churchill

"To change your life, you must first change your day."

- Unknown

"Success is no accident. It is hard work, perseverance, learning, studying, sacrifice and most of all, love of what you are doing or learning to do."

- Pelé, Brazillian pro footballer

Tip: Find passion in what you're studying. When you love what you're learning, it becomes easier to stay motivated and dedicated.

"You may encounter many defeats but you must not be defeated. In fact, it may be necessary to encounter the defeats, so you can know who you are, what you can rise from, how you can still come out of it."

- Maya Angelou, American civil rights activist and poet

"Make sure your own worst enemy doesn't live between your two ears."

- Laird Hamilton, surfer

"Good things come to people who wait, but better things come to those who go out and get them."

- Unknown

"If people only knew how hard I've worked to gain my mastery, it wouldn't seem so wonderful at all."

- Michelangelo, master sculpture, painter, architect and poet

"Work so hard that one day your signature will be called an autograph."

- Unknown

"I find that the harder I work, the more luck I seem to have."

- Thomas Jefferson, 3rd US president

"The only place where success comes before work is in the dictionary."

- Vidal Sassoon, hairstylist and philanthropist

Tip: Remember that hard work and consistent effort are key to achieving your academic and career goals. Keep pushing yourself.

"Successful people are not gifted. They just work hard, then succeed on purpose."

- Unknown

"Believe you can, and you're halfway there."

-Theodore Roosevelt

Tip: Cultivate self-belief and confidence in your abilities. Positive self-talk can help you overcome doubts and stay motivated.

"Striving for success without hard work is like trying to harvest where you haven't planted."

- David Bly, American politician

"Winners will fail over and over again until they succeed."

- Unknown

"I'm not telling you it is going to be easy —
I'm telling you it's going to be worth it."

- Art Williams, insurance billionaire

"Be stronger than your excuses."

- Unknown

"The man on top of the mountain didn't fall there."

- Unknown

"When we are no longer able to change a situation we are challenged to change ourselves."

- Viktor Frankl, neurologist, philosopher and Holocaust survivor

"There are two kinds of people in this world: those who want to get things done and those who don't want to make mistakes."

- John Maxwell, author and leadership expert

"Don't say you don't have enough time. You have exactly the same amount of hours per day that were given to Helen Keller, Pasteur, Michelangelo, Mother Teresa, Leonardo Di Vinci, Thomas Jefferson, and Albert Einstein."

- H. Jackson Brown Jr., author

"Success is stumbling from failure to failure with no loss of enthusiasm."

- Winston Churchill

Tip: Embrace setbacks and failures as opportunities to learn and grow. Maintain your enthusiasm even when faced with challenges.

"I've failed over and over and over again in my life. And that is why I succeed."

- Michael Jordan, former pro basketball player and businessman

"The difference between ordinary and extraordinary is that little extra."

- Unknown

"Success is the sum of small efforts, repeated day in and day out."

- Robert Collier, self-help author

"Work as hard as you can and then be happy in the knowledge you couldn't have done any more."

- Unknown

"The day you take complete responsibility for yourself, the day you stop making any excuses, that's the day you start to the top."

- O.J. Simpson, former American football running back

"Procrastination makes easy things hard and hard things harder."

- Mason Cooley

Tip: Combat procrastination by breaking tasks into smaller, manageable steps and setting deadlines for each. Use time management techniques like the Pomodoro Technique.

"Nothing is impossible. The word itself says 'I'm Possible'."

- Audrey Hepburn, actress and humanitarian

"Do the best you can until you know better. Then when you know better, do better."

- Maya Angelou, American civil rights activist and poet

"Rule no.1 is: Don't sweat the small stuff. Rule no. 2 is: It's all small stuff."

- Robert Eliot

"Failure is the opportunity to begin again more intelligently."

- Henry Ford, industrialist founder of the Ford Motor Company

"You have three choices: give up, give in or give it everything you have got."

- Unknown

"You don't have to be great to start. But you have to start to be great."

- Unknown

"The secret of getting ahead is getting started."

- Mark Twain

Tip: Overcome procrastination by taking that initial step. Once you start, momentum often carries you through the task.

"If your dreams don't scare you, they aren't big enough."

- Muhammad Ali

"If you really want to do something, you'll find a way. If you don't, you'll find an excuse."

- Unknown

"The thing about motivated people chasing their dream is they look crazy to lazy people."

- Albert Einstein

"We generate fears while we do nothing. We overcome these fears by taking action."

- Unknown

"Success isn't overnight. It's when every day you get a little better than the day before. It all adds up."

- Dwayne Johnson, actor and former pro-wrestler

"If you can imagine it, you can achieve it. If you can dream it, you can become it."

- William Arthur Ward

"The goal is to die with memories not dreams."

- Unknown

"The expert in anything was once a beginner."

- Helen Hayes

Tip: Understand that everyone starts somewhere. Don't be discouraged by initial challenges; they are part of the learning process.

"Failure doesn't mean the game is over, it means try again with experience."

- Len Schlesinger, Harvard Business School professor and author

"So many of our dreams at first seem impossible, then they seem improbable, and then, when we summon the will, they soon become inevitable."

- Christopher Reeve

"The people who are crazy enough to believe they can change the world are the ones who do."

- Steve Jobs

"A system is only as effective as your level of commitment to it."

- Unknown

"Doing things properly in the first place is the best way to be more productive later. You simply have less to do."

- Unknown

"Your education is a dress rehearsal for a life that is yours to lead."

- Nora Ephron

Tip: See your education as an opportunity, not an obligation. Visualize how your studies will equip you for a fulfilling and successful future.

"Infinite striving to be the best is Man's duty; it is its own reward. Everything else is in God's hands."

- Mahatma Gandhi

"Productivity boils down to two steps: identify the essential, then eliminate the rest."

- Unknown

"What we truly need to do is often what we most feel like avoiding."

- Unknown

"You were born to win. But to be a winner, you must plan to win, prepare to win and expect to win."

- Zig Zigla

"If you fell down yesterday, stand up today."

- H.G. Wells, English writer and sci-fi author

"Focus on being productive instead of busy."

- Unknown

"Keep your eyes on the stars, and your feet on the ground."

- Theodore Roosevelt

Tip: Dream big but also stay grounded in your approach to studying. Balance ambition with practicality.

"The secret of success is to do the common things uncommonly well."

- John D. Rockefeller, widely considered the richest man in modern history

"All the water in the sea can't sink a ship unless it gets inside the ship. Similarly, all the negativity in the world can't get you down unless you allow it inside you."

- Unknown

"If we wait until we're ready, we'll be waiting for the rest of our lives. Start now."

- Unknown

"Many of life's failures are people who did not realize how close they were to success when they gave up."

- Thomas Edison, businessman and inventor of the phonograph and electric lamp

"Worrying doesn't take away tomorrow's troubles. It takes away today's peace."

- Unknown

"You don't learn to walk by following rules. You learn by doing, and by falling over."

- Richard Branson

"The only limit to our realization of tomorrow will be our doubts of today."

- Franklin D. Roosevelt

"The whole purpose of education is to turn mirrors into windows."

- Sydney J. Harris

"The future depends on what you do today."

- Mahatma Gandhi

Tip: Keep your long-term goals in mind and remind yourself that your current studies are building the foundation for your future success.

"A life spent making mistakes is not only more honorable, but more useful than a life spent doing nothing."

- George Bernard Shaw

"You may see me struggle but you will never see me quit."

- Unknown

"Insanity is doing the same thing over and over again, but expecting different results."

- Albert Einstein

"Great things never come from comfort zones."

- Unknown

"Don't let the fear of failure be greater than the excitement of success."

- Unknown

"FEAR – Forget Everything And Run… or… Face Everything And Rise. It's your choice."

- Unknown

"People always say that I didn't give up my seat because I was tired, but that isn't true. I was not tired physically… No, the only tired I was, was tired of giving in."

- Rosa Parks

"Success doesn't come to you, you go to it."

- Marva Collins, American educator

"One of the most common causes of failure is quitting when one is overtaken by temporary defeat."

- Napoleon Hill, self-help author

"Remembering you are going to die is the best way to avoid the trap of thinking you have something to lose."

- Steve Jobs

"Don't watch the clock; do what it does. Keep going."

- Sam Levenson

Tip: Focus on the task at hand rather than constantly checking the time. Break your study sessions into manageable chunks and stay committed to completing them.

"I gave myself permission to make mistakes. I wouldn't ever give myself permission not to try."

- Steve Pavlina

"You cannot swim for new horizons until you have courage to lose sight of the shore."

- William Faulkner, writer and Nobel Prize laureate

"Don't stop until you're proud."

- Unknown

"Allow yourself to be a beginner. No one starts off being excellent."

- Unknown

"Power's not given to you. You have to take it."
- Beyoncé, 100 million record selling artist

"Be so good they can't ignore you."

- Unknown

"There are no secrets to success. It is the result of preparation, hard work, and learning from failure."

- General Colin Powell, former US Secretary of State

"Success consists of going from failure to failure without loss of enthusiasm."

- Winston Churchill, former Prime Minister of the United Kingdom

"Your time is limited, don't waste it living someone else's life."

- Steve Jobs

Tip: Stay focused on your own goals and aspirations. Avoid comparing yourself to others, as it can be demotivating.

"Believe in yourself and all that you are. Know that there is something inside you that is greater than any obstacle."

- Christian D. Larson

"Quality is not an act, it is a habit."

- Aristotle

"The earlier you start working on something, the earlier you will see results."

- Unknown

"The only way to do great work is to love what you do."

- Steve Jobs

Tip: Choose a study field or subject that genuinely interests you. If possible, relate your studies to your personal interests and career aspirations.

"However difficult life may seem, there is always something you can do and succeed at."

- Stephen Hawking

"Do what is right, not what is easy."

- Unknown

"It's not because things are difficult that we do not dare. It is because we do not dare that they are difficult."

- Seneca

"Most of the things you worry about never even happen."

- Unknown

"The person you will be in 5 years is based on the books you read and the people you surround yourself with today."

- Unknown

"Genius is 1% inspiration and 99% perspiration. Accordingly, a genius is often merely a talented person who has done all of his or her homework."

- Thomas Edison

"The greatest enemy of knowledge is not ignorance, it is the illusion of knowledge."

- Stephen Hawking

"And why do we fall, Bruce? So we can learn to pick ourselves up."

- Thomas Wayne, Batman's Dad, in 'Batman Begins'

"Live as if you were to die tomorrow. Learn as if you were to live forever."

- Mahatma Gandhi

"Success is the progressive realization of a worthy goal."

- Earl Nightingale, author

"You are never too old to set another goal or to dream a new dream."

- C.S. Lewis

Tip: Embrace a growth mindset. View studying as a lifelong journey of learning and self-improvement.

"Education is the most powerful weapon which you can use to change the world."

- Nelson Mandela

"Education is the passport to the future, for tomorrow belongs to those who prepare for it today."

- Malcolm X

"You miss 100% of the shots you don't take."

- Wayne Gretzky

Printed in Poland
by Amazon Fulfillment
Poland Sp. z o.o., Wrocław

25506965R00128